ACKNOWLEDGEMENTS

I spent 26 years associated with New York Life Insurance Company, 23 years in training and developing sales representatives and managers. This book grew out of a desire to provide focused development for sales professionals, those young in tenure as well as those who have been around awhile.

My heartfelt thank you to two covenant friends, Dr. Randy Marshall and Frank Harman. Randy is my encourager and encouraged me to embark upon this writing adventure. Frank lifts me up with his joy for life. Both keep me focused on the Truth of life on this earth.

Thank you to John Gray, Ken Chadee, Greg Lavalle, Dwight Beck, Larry McCoy, David Van Buskirk, Bill Ulbrandt and Morris Sims. All have touched my life, career and contributed to my growth in the field of training and development. Thank you to The Old Southwest Trainers Study Group. I am fortunate to be a member and have learned from many amazing development professionals over the years.

My love and thanks to my wife, Karen. She has supported and at times tolerated my whims and some goofy ideas over our years together. She encouraged me during those times when the thoughts or words for this book just would not come to mind. Karen is an amazing women, wife, mother and grandmother.

Table of Contents

Introduction

You have embarked upon sales as a career or perhaps have been at it awhile. As you may be experiencing or perhaps relying on someone else's experience, it is a rewarding career financially and personally. Yet it can be highly challenging and at times downright frustrating. Since you have chosen to open the first pages of this book you must feel there is an issue or problem in the development of your career that you are in search of a solution.

Believe it or not, we are all selling something everyday. Selling our children on the importance of telling the truth, our spouse on why we have to take time at home for work or even selling our self on "why do I stick with this career". When you take time to think about it, these may be some of the most difficult sales we make or do not make.

The purpose of this book is to be a resource on how to develop and grow in a sales career. Providing the basics on how do you identify training problems and develop solutions to those problems.

A dear friend and mentor of mine challenged me a while back to pick a word to focus on for 12 months. It took three weeks of thinking, pondering and prayer to uncover my first word. The word that I received ... NOURISH. It had nothing to do with physical food. I was compelled to nourish people everyday in their lives and endeavors as well as nourish myself in my life and career. Those 12 months have passed. It was amazing what focusing on "nourish" each day for 12 months did. It changed me. I was more aware when interacting with family, friends and new acquaintances of what could I do or say to nourish them emotionally, spiritually, or relationally. It was interesting how I was nourished by the all of those people and how it changed some of my choices of even books to read. To sum it up in a word…Growth.

My word for the second 12 months was BELIEF and it was an eye opener. It created in me a higher level of self-confidence.

My current word is FAITH and it is a fascinating journey to this point. This brief book should nourish you in your career, strengthen your belief and your faith the career you have chosen is a noble one.

See More People

During the 23 years of my career in training, development and implementation with one of the largest mutual life insurance companies in the U.S., there were always sales people struggling with their career. Some were new to the profession, while others were of varying tenure. It was interesting to read notes or over hear accountability sessions between a sales person and his/her sales manager attempting to determine what was the problem.

The most common solution presented to the sales person's problem or problems by a sales manager was "you need to see more people". If this is the solution from your sales manager or you arrived at that conclusion on your own, my inclination is to tell you to WHOA! It is not the magic cure all. "See more people" comes to mind as a solution in a very specific situation, which will be discussed later.

The first question that comes to my mind when hearing that phrase is "What kind of people?" The word "people" is rather broad and ambiguous. To illustrate how inappropriate the phrase is as a solution in developing a sales person; is it tall people, short people, young people, old people, people in a specific profession, people in Fort Worth, people who wear ball caps, people who drive motorcycles and on and on. If "see more people" was truly the solution for an individual's sales problems then there is still more analysis and specificity needed.

When you finish this book you should be able help yourself or manager with improved development and analysis. You will be able to nourish yourself with proper development and help those who come after you in this marvelous career. Keep in mind, "See more people" is not a great solution to sales development issues.

For those with a sales manager who may have said to you, "See more people", most likely it is not the sales manager's fault for providing a mediocre developmental solution. Unfortunately, many field sales organizations take their best sales people, after only a couple years of successful "selling", and entice them into "sales management". Being successful at selling does not directly transfer to being a successful manager.

Typically, only few are successful as a sales manager and the remainder end up going back as a sales person or leaving the company or industry entirely.

Sales managers with limited tenure as a sales person seldom experienced extended trials and tribulations of few or no sales. They seldom had to determine on their own or need a "sales manager's" insight to work with them on how to identify a problem and develop an appropriate solution to the problem.

Sales managers are primarily trained to recruit-recruit-recruit new sales people. They have had a modest amount of training, if any, on how to help a sales person develop a successful career. Thus the knee jerk solution given to many sales people who are struggling…"see more people" or "make more calls".

When the career is not going as envisioned, people begin to worry about their sales career. An ancient book helps keep my worry, most of the time, in perspective. An excerpt says, "So do not worry about tomorrow; for tomorrow will care for itself. Each day has enough trouble of its own." You and I have plenty on our plate today, to be worrying about tomorrow.

The great American author Mark Twain captured it when he said, "I am an old man and have known a great many troubles, but most of them never happened." Think about it. How many times have you worried about something which might happen tomorrow or even further in the future and IT NEVER HAPPENS!

Within the book there is information to use as a resource for when you need help and to keep your worries to those of today.

So what is the first action item?

This is your career. Step up and take ownership!

Let's get started on how to help you in this highly rewarding career.

Belief

First item to consider is BELIEF.

What is belief? A simple definition is trust, faith or confidence in someone or something.

Belief is grounded in the WHY you do what you do as a sales person. People buy from you based on you clearly communicating WHY you do this. If you go to my website (www.davidalyons.com) you will see on the opening page my WHY. Right up front for everyone to see quickly. The processes (how) and the product or products (what) you are representing are secondary to the WHY.

Belief covers many areas in a sales career or any career.

- Belief in yourself and your abilities
- Belief in the company you represent
- Belief in the product(s)
- Belief in the systems you use
- Belief in the people assigned to help you develop in the career
- Belief in your personal support systems (those close to you outside of the career)

You will probably think of others. Whether this list is enough for you or you add to it, there is a significant quantity of belief needed in a sales career.

Belief is the foundation upon which you must build. This will take some serious time to get inside your head and your heart and find out "Do I BELIEVE in….?" If a strong belief in what you are doing is not there, stop reading right now and take a few days away. You need to evaluate whether sales, as a career is truly where you need to be making a living. Not everyone is going to be successful as a sales person. If it were simple and easy, everyone would be in the career and compensation/commissions would be a lot less for sales people.

Let's touch on four beliefs at the top of my list.

Belief in YOU

Belief in your self is foundational. As with any structure it must begin with a solid foundation. You cannot build a stable structure or career on shifting sands or mushy boggy ground. You must have faith and confidence in you. You may be with a large sales organization or your own sales business, ultimately, it is you in the trenches every working day. You earning an income to support you, your family, your future desires. A strong belief in you and the abilities you bring to the career leads to knowing the WHY, solid self-confidence and commitment.

When you have difficulties with belief in you, here is a simple and helpful process. Sit down in a quiet area with a pad of paper and pen. Begin listing all your accomplishments. It doesn't matter whether every one applies to your career or not. Just begin listing them. You will be surprised how long the list becomes and how it lifts your faith in your abilities.

Norman Vincent Peale said, "Believe in yourself! Have faith in your abilities! Without a humble, reasonable confidence in your own powers you cannot be successful or happy."

Belief in your personal SUPPORT system

I have found this to be almost as important as Belief in You. What happens during the time outside of a career can be extremely motivational or beat a person down.

To come home to a significant other and immediately begin hearing negatives about the career you have chosen can be brutal. At some point most of us are going to throw up our hands and say, "I give up!" Sometimes our desire to stick with the career may cause us to attempt to put at the back of our mind the negative input when we walk through the front door of our home. This may strain the relationship to a breaking point.

Hopefully, before you embarked upon a sales career you and your significant other or if no one currently is that special person, you at least sat down with a close friend or family member to discuss the career. Too often individuals come into the career with "rose colored" glasses or more appropriately "green" as the potentially large financial rewards sometimes get in the way of reality.

A good friend of mine summarizes it this way. We begin with the "ideal", move to the "real" and end up with an "ordeal" and begin looking for a new "deal". We need those outside voices to help us understand the "real". Those who know us well are a valuable resource whether you are contemplating a sales career or any time during a growing career.

A sales career is not easy. There are amazingly great days, challenging days and days you will feel lower than a snake's belly in a wagon rut. You definitely need someone at home or a close friend to give you strength and support because at the end of each workday there is not a jubilant ticker tape parade awaiting you.

If your belief system allows, another personal support system is spiritually based. What ever your belief system, most encourage some time for prayer or introspection. It can be a breath of fresh air in times of despair and distress. At a bare minimum, find time each day, preferably in the morning, to read or listen to something motivational or inspirational to begin the day.

One of the U.S. founding fathers, Benjamin Franklin said it well, "Work as if you were to live one hundred years. Pray as if you were to die tomorrow."

Belief in Your SYSTEM(s)

The company whose products you are asking people to buy has spent significant time developing the sales systems to support their sales people. The processes you are trained to implement are time tested and proven to work for the company.

It is amusing how many people come into sales with no previous experience or limited sales experience and all of a sudden they know a better way than how the company has trained them. Sales systems work when you make them a habit in your business!

In *'The Power of Habit: Why We Do What We Do in Life and Business'* by Charles Duhigg, he writes:

> "It is belief, however, that I think is the most important aspect of creating positive habits that will lead to success…"

"When working on changing your habits, belief is crucial for getting you through the difficulties, speed plateaus or academic challenges."

Believe in what you are being trained to use and make t hem into habits. If it didn't work the company would have changed it before you ever walked through the door.

Once you get your feet on the ground and have a proven track record then if you think you need to tweak it to better fit you…fine. Until then put the blinders on and implement what you are trained to do.

How long should you stick with it. A rule of thumb says it takes 21 days for something to become a habit. 90 days is my general rule. Use it for 90 days exactly as you learned it. At the end of 90 days, if it isn't quite working for you then go to your development or training manager and ask for help. What you will most likely determine is that you were not using the process as you were trained. Commit to another 90 days and see what results.

A colleague, Tim C. FitzGerald, uses what appears to be a simple system. In general, the system is "book two appointments" each day, Monday through Friday, for some time in the future. Simple. Under the surface it has other components that are critical to it working successfully. You must know and use the entire system to be effective. Tim and his team use it habitually in their successful careers.

Those who take the time to learn the entire system, believe in it and implement it consistently are more successful than those who only see the "two appointments" portion. As Tim calls it, "Success, One Day at a Time".

Systems take the pressure off you if you learn them well and implement them consistently. When you make a decision to "wing it", your mind is more focused on what to say next than listening to and watching your prospect. Listening and watching are critical. Ninety one to ninety three percent of a message is tone of voice and body language. The words account for the remaining percentage of the message. If you are "winging it" then what are you missing in the message your client or prospect is attempting to communicate to you! Give yourself the advantage by mastering your systems and making them into habits.

Belief in your PRODUCT

Spending much of my adult life in the insurance industry, I always heard "you can't sell what you don't own." It makes sense. How can you effectively represent a product, you are not willing to buy yourself? Thus, I own various life insurance, annuities and mutual funds.

If you own a product, you most likely know more about the features and associated benefits of the product than if you did not own it. If your product is heavy construction equipment such as graders and bulldozers it is probably not possible to buy a couple of those to keep in your garage to use every weekend. Would be fun though! There are alternatives such as in the bulldozer example your company may have a location where you can actually use a demonstration bulldozer. By doing so, you know more about the product.

Let me share an example, not related to insurance or a piece of equipment. My family and I love to vacation on the panhandle of the Gulf Coast of Florida. We have been vacationing in one particular area for over 27 years and even today continue to explore the surrounding area. It never fails we always find someplace new we have not encountered in all the previous years. We have not bought a home in the area, although highly tempted several times.

Karen and I have "bought" this is the best place ever for our family vacations which now include our grandchildren.

Since I know the WHY of my passion for the area and am mentally invested in the area (own the product), my descriptions and stories, "features and benefits", are more impassioned when sharing with others. Friends have told me the Chamber of Commerce should hire me as an Ambassador for the Florida Panhandle area as I am selling it all the time! By the way, I live in Texas.

Get the passion for and believe in the product or products you are asking people to buy. You have to be red hot to get your prospect even close to warm.

Those are my top four.

Belief in You and your abilities. Belief in Your personal Support System. Belief in Your Systems. Belief in Your Product.

It is ultimately about having Faith. You can replace "belief" with "faith" in all areas we have discussed. Have the Faith to Believe!

We have our foundation of Belief, now let's move to identifying development problems sales people may be facing when they are struggling or hit a slump.

Knowledge, Skill & Will

There are three areas to look at when trying to determine where the problem lies before attempting to design a solution

Knowledge

First is Knowledge. Do you have the knowledge you need? For example, if you are going to sell a candle do you know why you are selling this brand of candle? Do you know how to sell candles or all the important features and benefits? Or do you only know it is a candle made of wax and it has a wick to light.

A candle may seem simple. It might be important from your buyer's perspective to know why you sell that candle brand over another, what is your process, what kind of wax or paraffin? Is it a taper, pillar or tea light? Is it scented or unscented, slow burning, cotton wick or wood wick, on and on?

Do you need to know every piece of minutia? Probably not. You should know all the main features and benefits buyers might expect you to know. Never forget, it is better to tell your buyer you are not sure of a detail and will get the information for her. Remember earlier "don't wing it"? Don't be making something up to move the situation along. It is difficult and embarrassing to come back later, especially after the sale and explain you were wrong.

If the problem is a lack of knowledge or limited knowledge the solution has probably already come to you. Get the knowledge! Reading assignments, online study, meet with someone who has the knowledge and learn from her.

It does not end there. You now need someone to drill you on the new knowledge to be sure you have learned the information correctly. Be sure the person who you are going to drill with is knowledgeable and is correct about the topic. Problems will arise if your knowledge drill time is spent drilling incorrect information.

The following personal experience illustrates the point. I was transferred to an office and was having my first skill and drill product session with about 12 relatively new sales people. One of the topics was a rider for a life insurance policy. It is an important rider for a prospective buyer to consider when buying life insurance.

I asked for a volunteer to practice with me on explaining the value of having the rider on my daughter's policy. The volunteer being the sales person and I would be the prospect. The volunteer had been a representative for almost a year and doing well in the career. I set the stage and off she went on features and benefits of the rider. Two minutes in I stopped her. The one feature and benefit she was explaining was incorrect.

I asked the group what was wrong with her explanation. Dead silence. One gentleman raised his hand and said "I haven't heard anything wrong." Being one to drive home a learning opportunity, I asked the group how many agreed with him. All the hands went up. Oops. Someone had taught and trained them on a piece of knowledge incorrectly.

We took a break and I asked them to go to the literature room, find the specification sheet on the rider then return.

As we read through it, jaws dropped. They learned the correct information. They also learned to do some checking on their own. Take ownership. Own your business!

Even experienced sales people and managers may not always have the correct information. It never hurts to follow up with research of your own.

Knowledge of your product is important. As mentioned when discussing Belief, for many prospects they first want to know the WHY you do what you do. Experience has led me to this conclusion. The WHY must relate to do you truly care about helping them solve their problem or problems. What this means is don't immediately launch into your sales processes or into spewing all your knowledge about the product. Share your why and take the time to find out what is important to your prospect. Then you can ease into your processes and use only the knowledge necessary to provide a solution.

Once you have a good grasp of the knowledge you need then move on to the skills.

Skill

Do you have the Skill? It is awesome to know your why, your processes and product inside and out. Can you take the information and present it properly as a solution to your prospect's problem?

Where do you learn skills? Through skill and drill sessions provided by your company's development department, a successful colleague or videos. If you are on your own, then find someone who can practice with you on proper presentation techniques. It helps if that individual is familiar with your processes and product(s).

Practice, practice, practice. Do your practice in front of a mirror, with your spouse, with a company trainer or with a coach. Be sure when you practice, your practice is perfect. When you practice and mistakes are made, not corrected, then you most likely will make the mistake in front of your prospect. Let me share a personal example.

I was a competitive swimmer from age 9 through college. I still swim five mornings a week, but I can't call it competitive. After college, I coached age group swimming for 15 years. During practices it was not uncommon for some of my swimmers doing the butterfly stroke to only touch at the end of the pool with one hand. In a race the rule dictates a two hand simultaneous touch on turns and the finish. One hand is a guaranteed disqualification in a swim meet! I would stop them and explain, "What you practice in this pool and do over and over is what you are likely to do in competition. One hand butterfly touches will get you disqualified in a meet."

Never failed, at least one of my swimmers would get disqualified during a competition. For what...a one hand touch on butterfly turn or finish! Exactly what they practiced over and over.

My coaching experience has taught me "practice does not make perfect", "perfect practice makes perfect...99% of the time." It even applies to the sales people I coach today.

Do it right and be sure whomever is evaluating you holds you accountable to the perfect practice.

Will

So now you know the knowledge is there. The skill is being done correctly. What is left that can get in the way? It is the most difficult issue to fix…Willingness.

Are you willing to do what you have learned? The underlying problem here is a core human emotion – Fear. Fear can be debilitating in a sales career. It can be a fear from the past, fear of the present or fear of the future.

Allow me to share the most common "willingness" issue I have encountered with sales people… making phone calls. I have had people who learned the phone scripts, perfectly practiced the skill, able do it well with me and with others. When it came time for making calls to ask for an appointment with a real prospect, oh my goodness.

I have seen people look at the phone on their desk for 10 minutes before they picked it up to make a call. They would then stutter and stammer their way through the call, not get an appointment, hang up and stare at the phone for another period of time before making another call. That is fear! After an hour they were exhausted and had only made 5 – 7 calls.

It takes a lot of work to overcome a willingness/fear issue. Sometimes the fear or lack of willingness cannot be overcome. In the phone example previously it could be a fear from the past, a bad experience on the phone in a previous job. Perhaps it is fear of the present. Will the person on the other end even talk to me or yell at me? May be fear of the future, I got the appointment now I am frightened about how I come across face to face. For a lot of people it is a fear of rejection, fear of the present.

It becomes a mental conversation about is the prospect on the other end of the phone saying "no" to you as a person or "no" to an appointment regarding your product. As long as you are professional and polite during the call the "no" is typically about the appointment or product, not directed personally at you. Sounds like a simple conversation and easy to understand, yet many people continue to struggle with the phone. They get it done, but it is a highly stressful event for them.

Fear of the phone is only one area were willingness is involved. It can raise its troublesome head any where in a career. Let us look at a simplified process to determine a solution to a problem in our career.

In determining an appropriate solution to a development problem it is important to review three questions. Do you have the knowledge? Do you have and can you perform the skill required? Are you willing to do it or is there a fear to work through?

Going back to the beginning of this book and the "see more people" solution, it might be appropriate if the problem identified is you are only seeing one person a week and expecting to be successful. What might be the root problem if time is taken to dig deeper is a lack of quality prospecting. Perhaps not asking for referrals, introductions or not using social media to full advantage thereby impacting name flow.

The process of development, first identify the problem, second dig deeper to find the root problem. Then apply these:

Is it a knowledge issue? Is it a skills issue? Is it a willingness/fear issue?

Now develop your plan to address the issue or problem!

Goals vs. Desires

The first time I ever heard or saw the individual who would become a covenant friend and mentor was over 20 years ago. Dr. Randy Marshall was a keynote speaker at a national conference for sales trainers for New York Life Insurance Company. The title of his talk was Goals versus Desires.

What a wake up for me when he said… we have Goals all wrong. Wait just a minute! I was an athlete and all my coaches, even me when I coached swimming, set team goals and individual goals. You are going to tell me all these years I have it wrong. Yes, after listening to his presentation, I did have it wrong.

Next he really got my attention when he said understanding the difference can improve my mental health. I have always stressed about am I going to reach my goals, so less stress… tell me more!

I am not going to take you through Goals versus Desires[1]. Suffice it to say, I "believed" what Randy shared during that conference. I had copious notes to refer to from his talk. Next step was the skill of implementing it consistently. For me it was a "says easy, does hard" situation.

As with most things new you study and gain the knowledge and it moves from hard to "I got it". Then you have to actually "do" the task. It moves from the knowledge side of "I got it" to the "Do" side and initially it is difficult. After

---

[1] To learn more about Goals versus Desires, www.drrandymarshall.com.

some time of "doing" the task it becomes easy. Strange how that works in about anything new I undertake.

Although it took me awhile to put it to work in my career and personal life, it made a difference in both areas. One important piece of Goals versus Desires is focusing on those areas you have significant control. You can't focus on what you control until you determine what you desire. In other words, identify the end result (desire) and work backwards to determine what you can control (goals) to achieve the desire.

A simple example, I want to lose 15 pounds, my desire. What do I control, my goals? I can stop eating ice cream before I go to bed. I can eat more vegetables and fruits. Cut out half-pound bacon cheeseburgers with fries every day for lunch. I can exercise. Got it? Things I have significant control over become my goals.

Apply this to an annual sales objective given to you by your manager. Presume your sales objective is $350,000. The $350,000 becomes the desire. What do you control on a day-to-day basis to have a solid opportunity of achieving the desire. Quick to mind items are: prospects, phone calls to schedule appointments and sales presentation ability. You can probably come up with a few more. People ask me what about having a minimum number of appointments each week. You control initiating on the phone or face to face to schedule an appointment. You lose control once the conversation begins. Now someone else has a say in making the appointment happen…the prospect.

Whether you are with a large sales organization or your own small business, where you are the sales force, it is critical to be accountable. So how do you be accountable to your controllable sales activity and results and use it to help you grow?

Activity Data

We looked at three development areas, Knowledge, Skill and Willingness/Fears and each one or a combination can impact your business. So where do they apply in helping you develop in your sales career. You need to understand what you do as a sales professional. In order to accomplish that task you need some data to analyze and review. You need to keep records. Track specific activities and results related to a successful career. What should you track? Below are three broad categories of activities to monitor and be held accountable on a regular basis.

- Name Flow
- Activity
- Results

Remember previously an important point from Goals versus Desires is focusing on what you control. The areas you have significant control over should be what your goals are based upon. In sales there are areas you have significant, if not 100% control over.

The topics to follow are from a spreadsheet in the appendix. It is a tool to help you grow in the sales profession. The spreadsheet is designed with highly controllable items on the left. As you move to the right you have less control.

Name Flow

In any sales career if you have no one to call or get in front of then you are basically unemployed. It all begins with Prospecting. We need to break this general topic of Name Flow into smaller, controllable pieces.

Asked for Referrals

Referrals and/or Introductions are the strongest source of qualified prospects for any sales professional. Rather than being a cold contact you are relying on the trust relationship your referrer has with the person referred to you.

Too often tracking in this area focuses only on referrals obtained. To help in our identification of a problem in your activities it is important to know how many times you "asked for a referral". Let me ask you a question with an obvious answer, how much control do you have over "asking for a referral"?

If you came up with anything less than 100%, then go back a few pages, read up to this section again and answer the question. This is a 100% controllable activity. Only you can utter the words to ask for a referral or introduction. If you cannot then there is a Knowledge, Skill or Willingness/Fear problem that now needs a solution. To make it very simple, do you know it, can you do it, and will you do it. See how that works!

Providing you a referral or introduction process is not a topic for this book. There are numerous ones available and some very good books on the topic. A recent search on the Internet using "referred lead process" had 62,300,000 hits. I think you can find one that fits you and your system. Should you want help on this topic or any topic in the book my email address is at the back.

Referrals Obtained

Knowing the results of asking for referrals would seem to be valuable. This is an area where you relinquish some control. Do you know why? You have someone else involved in the activity. You have given up some control because you have little, if any, control over how the individual will respond to your request.

Not everyone is going to provide you referrals. You may have times when you obtain 15 from one person and the next five times you ask you only obtain 1 from each person. When you do obtain referrals no matter how many you obtain they are golden. Would it help your attitude in this business if you knew that every time you asked for referrals you averaged obtaining 3 qualified names?

It would definitely help my attitude, my business and my income. If you average 3 every time you ask then in a week (Monday – Friday) if you only asked once per day the result is 15 new names in your name flow. Take it one more step; presume you work 44 weeks per year. 15 times 44 equals 660 new people to approach where you have the power of the referrer's name when you contact them.

I do live in the real world of sales and lets say you were able to only contact 50% of them and 50% of those allowed you an appointment. The result is 165 appointments just from referrals. Knowing this information not only helps the attitude, it is critical when it comes to planning for your business. In this scenario it might be beneficial to your business to ask maybe two or three times a day.

So how does "do you know it", "can you do it" and "will you do it" apply? If you are averaging obtaining one referral each time you ask it may be the wording or tone in the way you ask. Maybe you are afraid to "bruise the fruit" (hurt the sale) by asking for more than the first name given to you. Perhaps you don't know how to overcome initial objections to obtaining referrals.

As you analyze and think back over the situations it will be evident where the problem lies and the next step is to devise a solution. Allow me to share a personal example.

In the first few months of my sales career referrals were not where they needed to be. I knew how to ask, I could do it and was willing to do it. So what was wrong? Nothing really, except I was settling for the first two or three names a client was willing to refer.

A senior sales representative gave me a suggestion. Simply ask, "who of the individuals referred to me is going to be the most challenging to get an appointment for a meeting." Once that person is identified place a star by their name on the list. Then ask my referrer, "Since this person is going to be a challenge, who else would you recommend I contact to replace the starred individual?" Invariably, one more name was obtained and usually a higher quality referral.

Someone with many more years of experience was willing to share a simple piece of "knowledge" to add to what I already knew. It fixed the problem. Never think you know it all in this profession, because there are things you know you don't know and then there are things you don't know that you don't know.

Personal Observation

Personal observation, an activity you totally control. Most of us have two eyes, two ears and mouth. In personal observation all you need to do is keep your eyes open to the world around you.

You see a new business getting ready to open, a moving van is unloading in a neighborhood, you read about someone's promotion in the local newspaper (online version for some of you). All may be potential prospects for your product or services.

Next listen! Your ears can find prospects for you. I am not saying eavesdrop! Every one of us has been at a social event, sitting in a restaurant or waiting in a line and overhears part of a conversation that catches our attention. I am not aware of any regulations or etiquette rules that forbids one from saying "I happened to hear your comment about being concerned with... Let me give you my card."

This happened to me the week after Thanksgiving. I was visiting my mother at the retirement living facility where she resides and we were discussing a loose tooth she felt needed attention. A gentleman and lady happened to walk by our table at the time of the conversation. The gentlemen took a few more steps and came back to us. He said, "I apologize for interrupting, but I overheard your comment about needing to see a dentist. I am a dentist. (handed me his card) I make visits here one day a month and would be glad to examine your mother when I am here in December if you are unable to get her an appointment with her regular dentist by then."

Made my day! My mother's dentist is usually fully scheduled and it is four or five weeks out before I can get her an appointment. Was the dentist who interrupted us selling? Darn straight, selling his service as a dentist and convenience of seeing mom where she lives. He had a solution to our problem. Mom and I were not offended at all by his interrupting our conversation. Because he took a moment with us after catching just part of a conversation he probably will have a new patient in the near future.

Finally, your voice emanating from your mouth. Sounds strange, but unless you totally freeze up when someone speaks to you, you engage in conversation every day. Think about the last event you attended and it was not business oriented.

When you were introducing your self, "Hi, I am Dave Lyons". Usually questions follow such as, do you live nearby? How do you know so and so? And 9 out of 10 times somewhere in the conversation comes the question…"What do you do for a living?" Wham! What do you say? You better have something.

During my time in the life insurance business I heard a lot of things. I am a financial planner, I help people with their long-term goals, I help people fill holes in their financial program (that individual had a "hole" punched in his business card), and I provide cash to people when they need it most. My response, even when I moved into management, "I am a life insurance agent." Were there times when people took a step back as though all of a sudden I had extreme body odor? Yes. Other times, it led to an exchange of contact information and an appointment. As a manager, I referred them to an agent.

Be proud of whatever type of sales profession you are engaged. There is no reason to sugar coat it with some ambiguous description of what you really do for a living.

Other Controllables

"Other" is a broad category that can fill a book. Activities include, social media, direct mail, events, seminars, networking, associations, volunteering, civic groups, a website, drop in cold calls and on and on. These are all forms of marketing and prospecting. The more often you get your name and your product in front of people in a favorable format the better off you will be.

Social media is an ever-expanding place to market you and your products. If your product(s) are regulated by governmental organizations, what you can put on social media needs to typically be approved or supplied by your corporate compliance department.

There are numerous books pamphlets today with ideas and processes on how to make best use of social media in your prospecting and marketing process.

The same compliance issues come up for most items you put in front of the general public. Check with your marketing department before embarking on any of these methods. If you are a sole proprietor then I suggest at a minimum run it by your legal advisor for an opinion. Having some items that are automatic or take very little time to put your name and product in front of people is invaluable.

All of the items discussed you have total control or to a very high degree. Remember the key to succeeding, as a sales professional is focus on what you control!

Activity

The name flow items previously discussed are separated from this next area. Name flow is critical to a sales professional. Without name flow or prospects you have no reason to do all the other activities of the profession discussed below.

Most sales positions, other than a sales clerk in a retail store, involve being on the phone to contact prospects. Let's start there.

Phone Calls

Lets break phone calls down into a few smaller items to record for the data tracking.

Conversations

Conversations are initiated by you when phone calling. The sole purpose of the phone call should be to get an appointment. Guess what…it is controllable. You control whether you pick up the phone and dial someone's number.

Once done with the dialing you begin to give up control. The person called my not pick up, it could go to voicemail or even be a bad number. Those you cannot control. What you need to count are the people where you actually had a conversation.

A conversation is a two-way event. If all you got out was "Hello" and about three words of your phone approach and they hung up on you, don't count it. A friend of mine used to call these people immediately back and apologize that his phone cut out and dropped the connection, then start into his approach once again. He had fun; many people still hung up the second time. Yet some let him continue and he got some appointments. To repeat, a conversation needs to occur to count in your data tracking.

Some of you are probably asking…what do I say on the phone? Answer is it depends on what your company wants you to say. Also regulations come into play. Some states require you identify yourself, your company and if a state license is required to sell your product, provide your license number. My recommendation is use the phone approach provided by your company.

Sometimes phone approaches get "wordsmithed" to the point of confusion. You may have to modify some words if those words are not commonly used by you in a normal conversation. Your management or product supplier can help you with those modifications.

Along with knowing your phone approach be prepared to respond to objections. You will get them. How you respond will determine whether the conversation continues or not. A classic simple response is "Feel, Felt, Found".

Generally it goes like this, I understand how you feel, other people I have spoken to have felt the same way, what they found when we got together was… You fill in what they found with a benefit linked to the objection that was given. There are many other ways to respond to objections and many books written on the topic. Ultimately, remember the sole purpose of the phone approach is to obtain an appointment, not sell your product.

The next item to track is your appointments obtained from your phone activity. Simple, you either booked an appointment from the phone conversation or you did not.

The next item to record is a Callback. For every "Yes" you get to an appointment the remaining conversations do not all end in a "No" to an appointment. People will ask you to call back. Usually it is a timing issue. Perhaps the decision maker is not at home, they are getting ready to go out the door or sitting down to family dinner or just an inopportune time for them to have a conversation.

You may find in tracking appointments and callbacks, combined they far exceed the "No" to an appointment. Callback is an item on the tracking form, but you must have a means to record who and when to callback. You can easily do that with most calendaring systems or client /

prospect management systems available from your company or available through retail software outlets. You must have a system so the callbacks do not fall through cracks. You would hate to lose one and it could have been the one to make your year.

A friend of mine is highly focused in his business on the prospect and client. It seems like a small item, yet he will never ask a prospect or client to call him back. Think about how you feel when you leave a message for someone to call you back and they don't call back! Do thoughts come to mind such as, they don't like my product, they don't like me, or they weren't worth contacting? Guess who these thoughts are about...YOU!

Successful sales professionals are client centered, not self-centered. Remember one big takeaway from Goals versus Desires was control. If you ask them to call you back, YOU gave up control. If the prospect or client asks you to call them back in a week or month or after a holiday that is fine you are still in control.

Not every conversation is on the phone. A large number are conducted face to face. Earlier, there was the example of a conversation at a social gathering. If it led to a conversation about what you do, you obtained contact information, count it in your activity tracking.

Face to Face

There are only two pieces to track in face to face. One is "Total" and the other is "New".

Total Face-to-Face is how many people did you meet face to face and the conversation was about your product, your business and how it may solve a problem for the individual. Included in total can be second appointments, appointments to deliver the product, maybe a service appointment or an appointment to obtain referrals or introductions.

New Face-to-Face is how many of the people this week did you meet face to face for the first time. Our example of the conversation at a social event would fall into this category.

We now move to Initial Appointments.

Initial Appointments

These are the first appointments for a conversation face to face with your prospect to uncover problems and perhaps provide solutions. First, lets divide these Initial Appointments into two categories.

Booked

Booked Initial Appointments are those you booked to your calendar whether it was scheduled via the phone or face-to-face. It might be a 15 minute introduction appointment over a cup of coffee or it might be substantially longer. The key is your prospect and you agreed to a specific date and time to get together.

As you have experienced not every booked appointment is kept. Some people are courteous and call to postpone, reschedule or at worst cancel totally. Others just are not there when you arrive.

I recall going on an appointment early in my career and this is significantly before cell phones. The appointment was out in the country in Northeastern Indiana. I pulled into the driveway and just before I got out of the car the house lights went out. I walked up to the porch. I knocked on the door, no one answered. I stood there for a moment and noticed the curtain in the window move slightly. Knocked again.

No answer. I walked back to my car, drove down the road to a gas station, dropped a quarter into the pay phone and called my prospect. They answered! I told them I must have just missed them and so glad they were home. I would be there in 5 minutes and I hung up. I drove back, walked up to the darkened house. Knocked, no answer.

It was a Booked Appointment and never moved beyond that point. Oh well, I got home earlier than my wife had expected that evening.

Completed

From booked in your calendar to actually conducting an initial appointment and to count it as completed. This may seem minor. In analyzing your activities knowing what percentage of your initial booked appointments actually are completed can be helpful in future business planning. Keep in mind, completed appointments does not mean your prospect decided to buy. It could have resulted in a purchase or agreement to a second appointment or an end to the process with no purchase.

Solution Appointments

These are appointments where you intend to present a solution to your prospects problem. Once again we are dividing these into "Booked" and "Completed". A "Booked" solution appointment is a second or third or more appointment booked to gather more information and/or present potential solutions.

A "Completed" solution appointment does not require the prospect to buy to be counted. As long as you presented your solution and the appointment was concluded, that is what counts.

An important point to keep in mind, it is possible to have an Initial Booked Appointment, meet with the prospect, present a solution and have your prospect buy. All in one appointment.

How do you count all those pieces? Under "Initial", it would be one booked and one completed. You would also have under "Solution Appointments" one completed, even if the prospect did not buy. If the prospect did buy then you also record in the following topic – Results.

Results

Two items to monitor in this topic

Buys

Your prospect liked your solution to their problem or problems and made a decision to buy. A new client! In the tracking system this is recorded as "Buys" in the Results section of the spreadsheet.

As you have probably noticed within these pages I use "buy" or "purchase" instead of making a sale. The concept of helping people buy rather than you making a sale has a positive appeal.

Selling sometimes carries the connotation of pressure tactics to get your product to be purchased. Selling seems to be about you winning at the expense of your prospect or client. Buying is focused on the prospect or client and taking them through a process, which if done correctly, naturally leads to the conclusion…"I want to buy". It becomes a win – win scenario.

Commission

Finally, the one you were probably wondering if it would ever come up. Now after all the other items, how much did YOU make on what your client chose to buy? Commissions are important to your bank account and important to properly analyzing and planning your business. Commission is a desire, not something you have direct control over. As discussed earlier, focus on those items you have significant control and the desire (commissions) generally will be there.

Now what do you do with this record keeping? You must take time to analyze the information you are keeping. The analyzed information is highly beneficial.

Analysis

It is critical to keep accurate information daily and input the data at the end each week to the spreadsheet. Do not wait until the end of the week and attempt to recall what you did. Record the data daily on a separate page, day timer, or whatever type of daily calendaring system you use. At the end of the week record the totals in a spreadsheet similar to the sample at the end of the book.

Don't make judgments on your business on a daily basis. There will be awesome days, good days and days you would love to forget about. Even though the spreadsheet records on a weekly basis, the same applies, don't judge your business on one week or two.

What do you look for when analyzing your numbers? Trends. A simple analysis you can do with a brief glance, are your numbers increasing, remaining the same, or decreasing. If the trend is positive you are probably doing things well in that particular area. If it is declining then it is an area to note and watch.

Accumulate 4 or 5 weeks of data, then sit down and take a high level analysis. Look for an item that truly stands out. Not only for being below what you want, also for being better than expected. You have to know the winners and the losers, so to speak.

If an item or items show up as a problem then you should apply the "do I know it", "can I do it", and "am I willing to do it" process. Don't be over critical at this early stage as you may be moving through a normal learning curve rather than a problem needing a solution. It takes some thought on your part and maybe advice from colleagues to determine if it is a problem or a learning curve. From there you will create a development plan to provide the solution.

When you take time off due to vacation, illness or company conference, note those in your system. When you begin to analyze and see a week that looks as though you only worked 2 days, it might be you truly worked only 2 days due to attending a conference.

What if your initial analysis indicates no real change positive or negative? First question, are you getting what you desire from the activity? If you are getting what you want from the activity, consistent numbers do not mean something is wrong. If you are not generating what you desire from those numbers then it is time to take one of those deeper looks at what you are doing. Be sure you know what you want from that activity, the desire. (flip back to brief introduction to Goals vs. Desires)

After 90 days, it is time do some detailed review and analysis of each area.

In coaching sales people, the form at the end of the book is the tool I use. It helps in designing development solutions. Specifically, from looking at various ratios it is possible to determine the following and more:

- Are you obtaining quality prospects?
- Are you improving in your approach skills?
- Are you improving in your closing skills?
- If you are setting appointments by phone, are your phone skills improving?
- Are you improving at obtaining introductions or referrals?

- How much effort are you putting forth in the career? (may seem odd, yet after all these years, it has become very easy to discern)

Before jumping to an erroneous solution to a problem in the analysis items above, here are additional items to consider in doing a detailed analysis.

Have you changed something in a controllable activity? Things such as, who you are prospecting, have you been focusing on another activity and neglected one, did corporate compliance, product revision, severe economic issue or government regulation force a change? All can impact a development plan as well as an overall business plan. If none of those are part of the identified problem, then you should apply the "do I know it", "can I do it", and "am I willing to do it" process. From there you will create a development plan to provide the solution.

Remember it is a plan and needs accountability, reviewed and adjusted, if needed, based on results.

Don't expect a development plan to fix a problem in a week or two. It may or may not. Most of the time, it will create incremental improvement and may take a month or more to reach the desired point. Patience is a virtue in this process.

Delayed gratification is typical in a sales career. Think about it. You identify a prospect and move him through your process hopefully to the point where he buys. Usually, that is not a one-day sequence. Depending on your product, it may be a week, a month or even a year to reach the buying point.

Development plans are no different; they take time to achieve the desired result. They also must be adjusted as you progress.

Another benefit of the tool in the Appendix is it aids you in planning from a business perspective as well as development.

Since you are tracking all of these activities including commissions, one business planning opportunity is to place a dollar value on an activity. You can take you total commissions at the end of a month or quarter then divide that by your activity total. Same can be done near year end.

A simple example would be determining the average value of each "Buy". If each "Buy" is worth an average of $1,500 of commission and you desire to make $150,000 in a year that means you need 100 buys.

The real planning and goal setting comes from taking that information and working backwards to those activities you have total or significant control. Determining goals such as:

- How many Asked for Referrals must you do daily to result in one buy?
- How many Phone Conversation must you have daily to result in one buy?
- How many Booked Initial appointments must be made daily to result in one buy?

Setting these types of goals, ones you control, tied to your activity system will give you a greater opportunity for success in reaching your desire. Significantly better than starting the year saying my goal is $150,000 and not knowing what must be done each day to get there.

Summary

My desire for you is to take the information contained with in these pages and use it to develop into a highly successful sales person. The beginning is BELIEF. Without the foundation of Belief you will struggle. This is an up and down career. You will need your Beliefs to help carry you through.

As you grow in the career keep in mind you have to know where you are going. You must have a Vision for your business. An ancient book specifically references this and says, "Where there is no vision, the people perish..." "Perish" comes from a Greek word and in translation means, "to lose" or "be lost". Start with a 3 year Vision and clarify what is the WIN at the end of year 3. Develop a 1 year strategy and in doing so think...steps. Then narrow your focus to a 90-day plan.

Why have a 90 day plan? 90 days gives you enough time to evaluate what you have put in place and see some results. At the end of the 90 days you can make some adjustments for the next 90 day plan, if needed. These 90 day plans should tie into the steps you identified in creating your 1 year strategy. Not having a plan equates to a phrase I have heard for many years...failing to prepare = preparing to fail.

Consider what Resources you are willing to invest in your development. There are four you should consider: money, time, energy and systems. All will be required of you in a successful development plan.

Money comes into development in several ways. You may have in your development plan to attend a sales skills seminar conducted by a nationally recognized provider. It might be to purchase books, cd's or dvd's to provide you "knowledge" or demonstration of "skills". You may come to the conclusion in your analysis of your development you need to hire a coach for 30, 60 or 90 days. When it comes to hiring a coach or finding a mentor keep in mind an old proverb, "when the student is ready, the teacher will appear". It really seems to work that way.

Allow me to share a couple thoughts on a coach. First, a coach is there to prevent or solve problems. A person looking from the outside in can usually see issues that you may not.

Second, a coach is working to increase your productivity. Increasing your productivity may mean the coach might have some harsh words for you at times. A coach who is rah rah all the time is not doing you any good or you are perfect all the time.

If you are doing great then should you be spending time, money and energy on a coach? Possibly yes. As I mentioned earlier, you hire a coach to prevent or solve problems. Top professional athletes whose skills are amazing have coaches. Their coaches watch for changes that may cause the athlete problems in the future. Even if you are at the top of your "game" having a coach may be beneficial.

Time is part of your development plan. The 90 day plan is a time piece in your development. Time is involved when you are deciding how much time you will devote to improving or gaining knowledge, practicing skills and analyzing your data to identify problem areas and appropriate solutions.

Time management is kind a misnomer. You can't make a 60 second minute into 62 or a 24 hour day into 25. What you can manage are the activities in the time you have each day. So that means evaluating what activities are important to your business and your development.

When it comes to energy it is more about when is your best energy level morning, afternoon or evening? What ever you determine is your best energy level period is where you need to focus the activities critical to your success. Remember these activities would be the ones you control.

My best time is in the morning. I am operating well until about 1 or 2 o'clock in the afternoon then I can feel my energy beginning to fade. You probably already have a feel for when you are operating at your peak.

Systems we touched on early in the book. They take the pressure off of you when you know them well and use them consistently. Systems are involved in prospecting, marketing, sales processes, follow up service and many other areas.

Find the systems that fit with your Vision, your Strategy and your Plan. The form in the Appendix is a system. It allows you to track and analyze your business regarding development and your 90 day plans. It can be a good accountability tool.

You need accountability to be successful with development or really any plan for your business. Find a mentor, study group or coach to help you. Proper development is not a "go it alone" proposition.

Don't skip what we discussed a few a paragraphs above, you must have a plan. Not a dream, a wish list, or "I hope to" thought. A true plan, whether it be in the area of training or development or even your overall business plan. It must be clear, accurate and relevant to your career.

You have chosen a noble and rewarding career…the Sales Professional. Be proud of what you do and achieve what ever you determine is your personal definition of success.

Keep this one thought in mind as your grow in this wonderful career -

"Don't be so busy making a living,

you neglect to make a life."

Need some help? You can reach Dave Lyons at

lyonscoaching@gmail.com

www.davidalyons.com

Appendix

ne here

Weekly Controllable Activity and Results Summary

Name Flow						ACTIVITY											RESULTS	
						Phone Calls			Face to Face		Initial Appts		Solution Appts					
Asked for Referrals	Referrals Obtained	Personal Observation	Other Sources	Total Names Obtained		Conversation	Appts	Callback	Total	New	Booked	Completed	Booked	Completed		Buys	Comm
				o													
				o													
				o													
				o													
				o													
				o													
				o													
				o													
				o													
				o													
				o													
				o													
				o													
				o													
				o